On Paper

Phibarilin Shangdiar

BookLeaf Publishing

India | USA | UK

Presentation by *BookLeaf Publishing*

Web: www.bookleafpub.com

E-mail: info@bookleafpub.com

ISBN: 9789363318885

First edition 2024

Missing You

I want to talk to you.
No, as a matter of fact,
I need to talk to you.
You make me feel calm and collected.

My tears are at bay when I talk to you.
Your annoying jokes,
Your irritating nicknames,
I miss them all,
And most of all,
I miss you.

I need you right now.
This heart-wrenching pain,
This uneasiness I feel,
Only you have the power to calm.

Yes, I pray
For guidance and strength.
But I need you.
Sometimes, I need only you.

How Does It Feel?

How does it feel,
To have someone DEFEND you,
Even when you're in the wrong?
How does it feel,
To have someone you love,
Yet your THOUGHTS wander elsewhere?
How does it feel,
To give in to TEMPTATION,
And SCARRING another human?

Your sensual nature,
Nothing to take pride in!
But so is my temper.
However, I shall continue,
To scream and shout,
For your actions are improper!
I shall not stay silent any longer,
For God's creation
Is scarred by temptation.

A Heart in Conflict

I'm confused,
Unsure,
Mentally drained,
Disoriented and disorganized.

My mind and soul are not at peace,
And I'm torn into pieces.

My brain wants you,
My heart wants another,
It's wrong, I know,
But there is nothing I can do.

It's funny, however,
Laughable to the least,
The people I'm torn between,
Have no intentions for me.

Words

She thought she needed closure,
And so she got it.
But words without measure,
May lead to disaster.

Things she wanted to hear,
He could not offer,
Ultimately leading to nothing,
But heartbreak.

It is said:
Actions speak louder than words,
But words hurt!
Words without thought,
Hurt a thousand times more,
Than a tiny physical blow.

Soulmates

Do you believe in best friends?
No, she answered,
I believe in soulmates.

Oh, how magical!
To have a bond
Connected by the soul.

How mystical!
Though it seems illogical
To be soul-tied to someone, be that friend or
lover.

The People I Trust

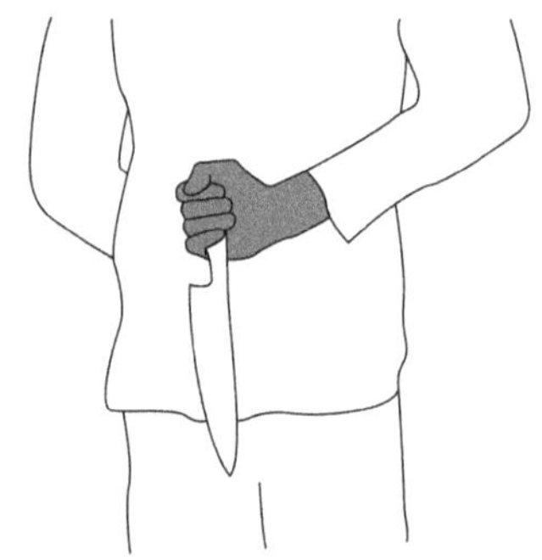

I shall not ask HOW
Or WHAT was the cause.
But all I say is WHY?
WHY did you have to stab me
Behind my back?
When I gave you NOTHING but trust
And a reason
For YOU to trust in me.
But instead of honoring
Our friendship,
You went behind my back
And LIED.

I was never weak.
It was just that my enemies,
Were the people I trusted most!

Just Misunderstood

Death is feared by everyone,
It seems.
Everybody tries to run away from it,
While some seek it
Only when life gets difficult
Because they think it'll give them peace.

I, however, think Death is just
Misunderstood.
He seems sad and teary-eyed.
He's lonely and with
No one to turn to.
Still it seems Death is beautiful.

People look at him with anger.
They resent him.
Thus he walks alone in the shadows
Of dark alleyways and crevices,
But when we think of it
It's only because of Death that life is
meaningful.

A Thousand Love Poems

Poetry, I never really liked it, never really hated
it.
The beauties of nature, the various works of art,
I lived ignorant of these.
Their existence I never once appreciated or
cared about.

But then I saw you and a thousand love poems
were all I heard.
Up to the point where I was scared—
Scared that I had fallen, not knowing how deep I
was to fall.
Frightened not knowing what lies beneath this
bottomless pit.

But I'm always scared.
Knowing no matter how much I wish for it,
No matter how many stars heard it,
In this bottomless pit of love, I had fallen a little
too deep.

Though knowing very well that over a thousand
years,
A thousand wishes,
A thousand lives,
You will never be mine.

A thousand love poems were all I could hear,
In this world of blabbering people,
A thousand love poems were all I heard,
Whenever you're near.

Unrequited Love

I broke my own heart by falling for you.
I knew what it meant to fall for you,
Yet I fell deeper and deeper still.

A ruined friendship,
A love story that never started
All because I chose to give my heart to you.

Hate me you say
But I say I can't.
For you are the best part.

And I hope and pray
And wish on every star,
For you to come back.
And this time, to never be apart.

Just Shut Up

Sometimes the BEST thing to do
Is to keep your mouth SHUT.
When there's nothing to say,
The best thing to do
Is to just SHUT UP!

Because most of the time,
The BASELESS MINDLESS words
That comes out of one's mouth
Makes another burn.

The flames of anger, at times controllable, yes
But most of the time they're not,
And words spoken out of anger
Cause a hundred times more injury
Than those that come out of an empty mind.

Sometimes we say I take it back,
But is it taken back?
Is it really gone from that person's head?

The truth is it never really is,
And the words given to another
Can never really be taken back.

Happiness and Peace

I wonder what would happen
If everyone disappeared,
And all this world alone to me belonged?
Would I be happy?
Would I find peace?

Free from all the day-to-day chaos;
Alone with nature's serenity,
And it's flora and fauna,
Untouched by no one but me.

Happiness and peace
I was sure to acquire,
But only for a short span of time,
For it's only a matter of time
Before I start missing
My dear ones.

The calm winds would not be able to keep me
still,
And the noiseless world
Would keep me up at night,
I'd be frightened of the dark,
The light and even of my own sight.

Happiness and peace
I was sure to acquire,
But only for a short span of time,
Before I go haywire.

Growing Up

As a child in a world of adults
I wanted to grow up,
And be like them
Carefree, with the freedom
To have all the fun in the world.
I would wake up each day,
And counted the days
To see if my birthday was soon to come,
But that was when
I was a child.

Now that I'm aging,
And growing up in a world
Of people who once upon a time
Like me thought that
Growing up would be fun;
I see that growing up
Is not all fun and games.
It's stressful, and it takes tact
To get by everyday
By putting on an act.

I do not count the days anymore
To see if my birthday was soon to come.
Now I spent the time,
When I'm not needed to pretend,

To sit back and reminisce
On the good old days.
When I was running barefoot,
Without any care.
When life was blissful,
When life was actually peaceful.

Home

What is home?
Home is not only a house.
It's family and loved ones
But a family full of fights,
Arguments and disagreements
Is not home.

Home does not leave one traumatized.
It does not drain out
One's will to live.

Home is safe
With a feeling of warmth,
And coziness
Attached to it.

Bottled Up

All bottled up inside,
And none lends an ear.
Broken and confused
Trying to heal,
And at the same time
Trying to let go.

One comes and goes.
Another comes
But this one, I should let go.
Friends, my pleasure,
And family, my treasure.
But none that I want
At my leisure.

Sadness and delight.
Happiness and pain.
Angry yet calm.
Every emotion hitting at once,
And every single emotion
All bottled up inside.

Wanting to let it out,
But no one to turn to.
The only thing left to do
Is to let it out
On paper.
To write every thought,
And let out every emotion.

Sleepless Nights

Its 3:00 am,
And I find myself staring
At the ceiling.
The clock ticking,
The room, in a state of total darkness.
I lay there alone
Wondering why I'm awake.
My mind, an empty vessel,
And my body drained.
What is keeping me up?
I know not.

Turning to the left
Then, to the right
Listening to songs of the night.
A momentary fright

Hid me under warm blankets
Then, the world starts to spin
And everything becomes irritable.
It's now 4:00 am,
And I know not
Why I'm still up.

Life's

I want to live, he said.
There's the future to look up to.
Life's been hard,
But optimistic,
He's ready to face
All the challenges life throws at him,
And live his life to the fullest.

I want to die, she said.
Who cares what the future holds!
Life's been pleasant,
But reality struck,
And left her in the dirt.
Though she learned to never give up,
She no longer has the desire to try.

The Same World Only It's Different

As I listened to the stories
My parents and grandparents
Told of their past;
I find myself wondering
At how life was
When they were young,
And how the world was back then.

A world without modern advancements.
A world where human interaction existed
Not only through screens,
But in direct contact.
Where people would sit together,
And be together
Instead of being together,
But so distant from one another.
A world where nature
Was still at its prime.
A world where man
Respected his creator.

A glimpse of that world
I did see,
But only a glimpse,

And there's nothing I wouldn't do
To go back to those days.
Though, nothing but a glimpse
I would gladly relive it all.

Another Me

It feels like I'm standing in front of a mirror
Staring at my own reflection,
But in reality
I'm looking at you.
The idea of you being the exact image of me,
Impossible though it may seem,
But when I look at you, I see
You're another me,
And I'm another you.

All Over Again

I do not regret meeting you,
Befriending you
Or even falling for you.
Though, we were never meant to be
I would do it all over again.

In every lifetime
I would search for you.
In every lifetime
I'll wait for you,
Befriend you,
And fall for you all over again.

The stars in the sky may never align,
And our story would always have the same
ending,
But in a heartbeat, I would do it all over again.
For in a thousand lifetimes
There might be one where you and I
Were meant to be.

2 months

The moon is beautiful, isn't it?
That's when it all started,
Then came the late-night calls,
The good morning and good night texts.
The usual meetups and
The pictures that filled my phone's gallery
Of places only we know.

I didn't know, however,
That it would end
Only after a single mistake.
What we had was not worth fighting for,
And other people's opinions were more
important than our love.
The good morning and good night texts
Were now forced,
And the jokes we once laughed at ceased to
exist.

You started it with,
The moon is beautiful, isn't it?
And I ended it with,
The sunset is beautiful, isn't it?

14 years

What is the biggest lie
You told yourself?
Mine was that you didn't exist.
I had spent my entire life,
Convincing myself that
We never met,
And managed somehow
To keep it up.
Moving on with my life
With new friends and new faces,
When you were always in the back of my mind.
But then as if predestined by the stars
We once again crossed paths,
And this time, old enough to understand.

As a child, I had no idea
What it was.
The uneasiness I felt when your attention
drifted,
Or the heaviness I felt when we said goodbye,
But now that I'm older
I know that it was love.
I loved you
Since I was a child,
Yet I managed to convince myself
That you never existed.

I don't know how,
But I just did.

However, when our paths crossed once again
I'm no longer able to lie,
And soon I fell,
Deeper than the first time.
I was frightened of it, no doubt,
But then you assured me by saying
That if I fell, you would be there to catch me,
But now I'm falling
And you're nowhere to be seen.
Call me, you said, when you're scared
And to tell you the truth, I am.
Every day I call out to you,
But you're never there.

The first time you left
I didn't care for what I felt,
But now
My heart yearns for you,
And I know not what to do.

Where My Thoughts Stray

Picked up my guitar to play,
But let my thoughts stray.
"To whom?" You may say.
For there are a million people
Whom I could've thought of,
It could've been anyone, for that matter,
But it's only to you
That my thoughts stray.

A Silent Goodbye

I realized something today,
And that is, one day,
Sooner or later,
I must let you go.
You'll be with the person you want,
And I can't stop that.
But all I can do is,
Stand and watch,
As "The One"
Makes her way to you,
To be with you
Forever.

Falling For a Friend

I'm tired of this.
One moment,
You're pulling me in,
And the next,
You're pushing me away.
I don't know what I did wrong,
Or when it came to this,
But I can't help it.

I like you.
I love you,
Even before I knew what love was.
And the fact that a single text from you
Made my feelings resurface,
After I had tried so hard to keep them in,
Is frustrating.

You keep saying that I don't listen,
But I don't know what you want me to listen to,
When you don't even say a single word.
And I find myself,
Forcing life,
Forcing my life,
But what difference does it make?

You're my best friend,

But it seems
I'm nothing to you.
You're constantly trying
To keep me out of the troubles of caring for you,
That you don't even see
That your actions
Are hurting me more than they should be.

You Never Left

From the moment
My eyes opened
You were there.
I didn't know who you were
Nor why you were there,
But since you never left
I figured I might as well
Just lean on you.

Never once did you let me down,
And I find myself
Always looking up to you.
You hid your anger
And always painted on a smile,
And at times when we fought,
You would make sure
That we always made up.

You never left,
And your influence,
Every day, I felt.
I find myself trying to live up
To what you are every moment of my life,
And when I was in need,
I knew exactly
Who to turn to.
A friend so dear,
Never have I found in anyone else,
But only in my brother.
Someone so irreplaceable,
Someone so near.

Books Here, There and Everywhere

Books here,
Books there,
Books everywhere.
The room is silent,
And only faint whispers
Can be heard.
Friends here,
Couples there,
Some actually studying,
While some are just there.
I am one of them,
I am just there,
Letting my eyes wander about,
Wondering what really goes on in their minds,
While staring at the SILENCE at the entrance
Of the library.

Is The World Bad?

Chaos here
Disorganization there,
What is happening to the world?
They say the world is bad
But is it really the world that is bad
Or is it us human beings
Who are turning it bad?
We do things to destroy nature,
And disrupt the way of the world
With the ever-growing knowledge
We think that we can play God
When in reality,
All we are doing is hurting our home
And ourselves.

Fear

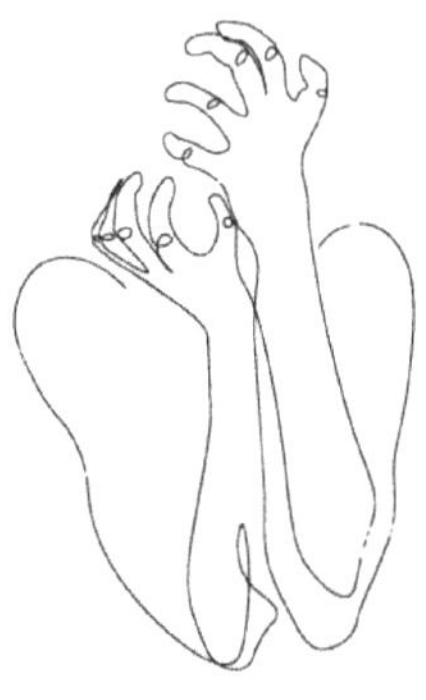

I can still feel my body shivering
My heart pounding still,
And my mind cannot comprehend.
This feeling
I know it all too well,
And it's been engraved
In every nook and corner
In every body part
And every cell.

Stargazing

Every time I step out
Into the darkness
And the moon and stars
Caught my attention
I wonder
Whether you're out too.
Staring at the beautiful starry night
I wonder
If you're stargazing too;
For even if we're miles apart
We could be stargazing together.

I promised myself
That I would let you go,
But to my disappointment
All my efforts
Were pointless.

For everyday
I find myself searching for you in every face I
see,
And every night,
The moon becomes a constant reminder of you.

Not Perfect

It's funny
How you're able to spot every single flaw in
others
Yet you fail to see your own.
You're not perfect either,
And maybe you know it all too well,
But instead of acknowledging
Your flaws and imperfections
You make yourself feel better
Or maybe even superior
By making someone else feel inferior.
You have no right to say anything
Be it about one's look, behavior
Or even life,
You aren't perfect, either.

Chasing Him

I saw Death sitting
Alone in a dark corner,
And I approached him.
He looked up and smiled at me.
I extended my hand,
But he refused to take it.
"It's not your time yet, my dear child,"
He said, stood up, and left.
I ran chasing after him
As fast as I could,
But could not catch up;
For it still wasn't my time.

World's Chaos

The quiet before the storm.
Nature is still at peace,
And everything was calm.
But then, out of the blue
Darkness appeared,
And enveloped the earth,
The breeze was no longer gentle,
The seas no longer still,
The world is in chaos
With darkness everywhere.

Losing Themselves

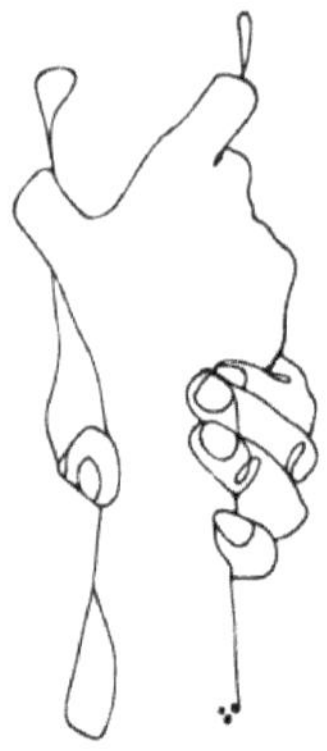

Stay! She begged,
Without realizing that
Each time she did,
She was losing a part of her.
She loved him too much,
And he loved her too less,
But to let go
Was not an option for both.
So painfully and angrily
They held on to each other,
Losing some part of themselves
Bit by bit, every day.

Even Amidst the Chaos

Suddenly, the air becomes thick
Too difficult to catch my breath.
The world starts to spin,
And I feel faint,
But even in the midst of all that
My mind still wanders
To you.

3 Roses

I only knew that red roses stood for love,
And other colors for something else,
But I was still delighted to get some from you.
Three roses you gave me
A different color each
However, I didn't know
That three roses meant
You didn't love me
Until my mother told it to me.

You

Only the moon knows
How much I think of you.
Only the stars know
How I long for you,
But only my pillows know
The tears I've shed
For you.

A Party!

Blabbering here,
Gossiping there,
And sitting in the middle of it all
Is pure torture.
I thought we were here to celebrate
A special day,
And not to make it about ourselves
By saying I did that, you did this,
They're like that, they're like this.
A party?
No,
But a place of constant blabbering and gossip.
There are so many places I could be.
Where? I do not know,
But I would gladly be anywhere else
Than here.

Wandering Thoughts

My heart is heavy,
And I know not why.
My mind is weary,
And I still don't know why.
A thousand thoughts ramble in my head
Telling me to do that;
Telling me to do this,
But in the end
I find myself wandering about
Aimlessly,
Without a thought,
And no clue of what to do.

Reading to Escape

Reality has taken a toll on her
Life has never been good for her
Yet she stays strong,
And brave as ever.
Then she found words,
Written on paper,
And they became her escape
From the world around her.

A Dream

She closed her eyes,
And flew to a place
Whose beauty was unimaginable.
A place of peace.
A place of joy.
A wondrous place,
But then she opened her eyes,
And fell back
To reality.

A Blessing or A Curse

What's a blessing for some
Is a curse for one.
A disadvantage for one.
An advantage for some.
Yet most tend to grumble,
And complain,
Without considering things
Sometimes as plain as day.

Still in the Past

My mind is still stuck in December.
My heart is still stuck in the years
That have long passed,
But my body has to be present
In the present,
Not future nor past.

It's a Crush, I Think

A crush was all it was.
I liked you not in that way,
But in the sense where
I aspire to be like you.
Though we're both from different worlds,
I still dream of a day
When I will come close
To be anything like you.

The First

You were the first, I thought.
I had come to love you so easily
That I forgot
You were just someone I knew.
Someone I met by chance,
And someone I chose to love
Because the person,
The first person I loved
Was nowhere to be found.

Patience, Rejection, Healing

To wait for someone is tiresome,
And requires patience,
But to have someone wait for you
Now, that's something else entirely different.
How hard did that person fall?
Even after years of rejection
Would pop up every once in a while
Back into your life,
But it doesn't matter
For when the hurt has healed
The love once shared is forgotten,
And a forced love
Is not love at all.

Bittersweet Memories

Our story was only
A short chapter
With a sad ending,
And a lot of
Beautiful memories,
Along with a lifelong lesson.

Love You Always

I cut my hair,
And washed away your scent.
I think I will always love you,
But you can no longer have me.
A day will come when you'll realize
That you loved me still,
But then it would be too late.
I will love you always,
But never more shall I beg
For you to stay.

Trapped Inside

It's burning inside
With every passing second
It seems like the heat refuses to go away,
But then outside, it rains.
It's cool and comforting,
Yet she cannot go out.
She's trapped in the heat,
Forced to bear it,
As it kills her slowly,
And painfully.

The Value of Time

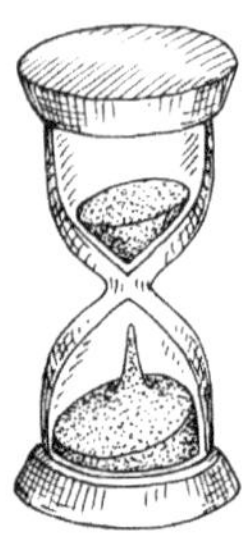

Every day in our lives, we keep saying
"I'll do it tomorrow."
We endlessly choose to procrastinate
Without thinking about the many dreams that
could've come true
The goals that we would've achieved
And the expectations that we could've lived up
to.

We procrastinate without knowing what
tomorrow might hold
What tomorrow might bring
Without knowing that
Every second, every minute, every hour
We spent doing nothing
We're one step closer to losing it all.

Seasons of Life and Death

Life is walking ahead of me,
And I'm trying so hard to catch up,
But the more I chase it
The more I find myself
Patiently waiting for Death.

Spring, the season of life, has come and gone,
And Winter's death is just on the horizon.
For a season so cold and cruel
Brings with it more joy and peace
Then all the others could.

The Silence Between Us

We still exist in each other's world somehow,
But we don't call
We don't laugh
We don't talk
Like we did before.
I would put up a random image,
And you would look at it, no doubt,
But you wouldn't reach out,
And as for me
I'm too frightened to even send
A simple "Hi".

When Nature Strikes Back

Funny to see how
The so-called courage and bravery
Of Man turns into pure cowardice
When Nature takes her chance,
And strikes back.
After Man has done all he can
To plunder and destroy
All its beauty,
All its gifts.

When Nature strikes back
It seems all Man can do
Is hide in the comfort of his home,
And hope and pray
That Nature's anger will soon end
Otherwise, he must prepare
For his own end.

Starting? No. Ending?

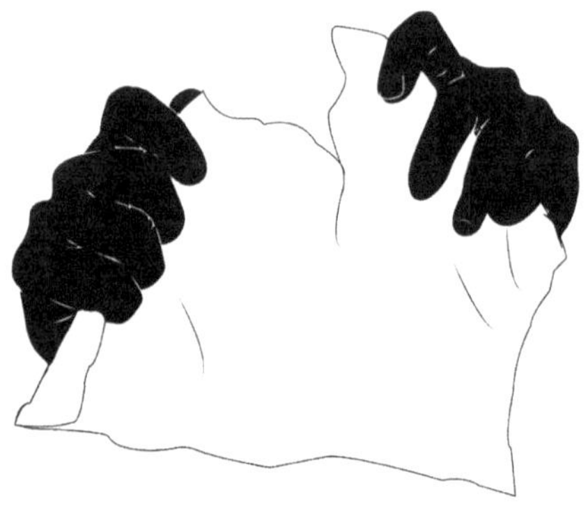

Milton, Wordsworth, Keats:
All these poets
All their works
I read and tried to understand,
Only to find myself failing miserably
To even catch
The point of starting,
And still confused
Even when reaching
The point of ending.

Lack of Patience

Patience is a virtue,
But what if
I do not have the patience
To wait.
Everything needs to be done,
Right this second.
I know it's wrong,
But it's something
I lack.
I care not how
Everything needs to be done
Right now.

Thoughts in the Waiting Room

Sitting in the waiting room
Packed with people
Doctors here, patients there.
The buzz of hospital workers everywhere.
The world begins to dance,
And home is all I can think of,
Warm and cozy,
Away from the noise,
Away from the crowd,
Alone in my room
With no one around.

Unsent Because of Fear

Messages typed,
But never sent.
Letters written,
But never posted.
Fear always gets the best of me.
Fear of what you might say.
Fear of angering you
For who am I to feel
These feelings I feel
Towards you.

Love and Letting Go

If you love someone
Let them go.

But why?
Why must I?
And that too just because of love.

Can I not love the person?
Without having to think
Of ever letting them go,
That is.

If it's meant to be
They'll come back,
And be yours to keep
Forever.

What if
I do not want to be
The person they come back to!

Why can't it just be me?
From the very beginning!
Why can't it be me?

If you love someone
Let them go,
And if it's meant to be
They'll come back,
And be yours to keep
Forever.

These words stuck in my mind,
And engraved in my heart.
However, a small part of me believes,
That if it was truly meant to be
I shouldn't have to give you up
Or let you go
In the first place.

My Mask

I'm shouting,
Crying,
Screaming at the top of my lungs,
But only on the inside.
On the outside, however
I'm putting on a smile,
Laughing,
And living.

Invisible Scars

He walks around in circles
While I'm stuck in the middle
Whether he's sober or not
I could not tell,
But all I could feel was my own fear.
One wrong move I feared
Would have a tragic ending
So I sat there
Shivering, praying,
And holding back my tears.

I have experienced this;
One too many times,
And till now I never liked it.
This person knows no boundaries

And when I tell, people listen
They only listen,
But do not hear.
I am left to fight it alone.
I am left to suffer alone.

Only praying won't help,
Especially when I'm not doing anything
To help myself,
But how could I?
He's in his what?
30s or 40s or 50s
Married and from a wealthy family
While I was only 14
When it began,
And still under the control
Of reputed people, yes,
But people who are
Too afraid to act
Because people will talk.

I have prints on my body.
Prints that I paint every day
With denial, sometimes love
But most of the time
With false happiness.

Your 20s

When you're in your 20s,
You have a lot on your mind.
You thought that by now,
You would've had your entire life
All figured out,
But in reality,
You're still struggling
Just to even make it
To the end of Today.

The thought of Tomorrow
Is troublesome,
And whether Tomorrow might come or not
You don't know.
It seems only Yesterday,
You were young
Only to find yourself
Much, very much older
Today.

I'm currently experiencing it.
The fear of Tomorrow,
The question if I would even make it
Till the end of Today.

I try to live in the moment,
To be in the Present,
But sometimes
I couldn't help but wonder
What lies beyond
The boundaries of Today.

My Heart, My Mind

My heart,
It feels like it's going to pop out of my chest.
My mind,
A total blur,
And the whole world
Though bright as day,
Is as dark as night.

Indifference

YOU DON'T CARE!
I had to figure it out the hard way.
I could be trapped,
Or I could've fallen,
Or I could even be hurt,
And you still wouldn't care.
My guess is that
You never did,
Or maybe I could be wrong,
And that at some point
You did.
But now
You don't.
You just don't care anymore,
Do you?

My Aching Heart

My heart aches.
I know it aches for you.
But I refuse to believe it.
I know it aches for you,
And only you,
But will never accept it,
Not even in my wildest dreams.

I'll let it ache.
I'll take the pain,
If it means making you stay.

Beauty: Life, Nature and Death

I'm beginning to see beauty in everything, it
seems.
Life: Its questions and mysteries.
Nature: With its various and glorious gifts,
And Death: The great denominator.
All these things
Have proved themselves beautiful,
But the one thing I can never find beauty in
Is Man.
His pride,
His vanity,
His greed,
They all make him
Less beautiful.

After The Storm

After the heavy storm,
The clouds finally part ways,
And the night sky is clear.
We stand outside,
And search for the stars.
One by one, they appeared,
And we never stopped to admire them.
Counting each one as they pop up in the clear
night sky,
We fail to notice the beauty of the crescent
moon,
Which stood there,
Staring at our faces.

A True Friend

Nothing hurts more than losing a friend.
I'm not saying that losing your lover doesn't
hurt,
But all I'm saying is that
Losing someone you trusted and loved hurts.
Losing someone who knew every dark secret
Every corner of your life hurts,
Especially when that friend feels like family.
Losing a lover is one thing,
But losing a friend
It's like being stabbed by someone
Who you thought was holding the knife to
protect you.

But real friendships formed over the years
Don't just break off easily over mindless and
nonsensical arguments.
A true friend would never think of hurting you,
And a true friend would always choose to stand
by you no matter the consequences.
A true friend,
Well, a true friend is special,
And holds a special place in one's heart.

Aimlessly Wandering

I'm home, yes,
But I don't feel at home.
I'm with my family, no doubt,
But I still feel the need for company.
I'm loaded with chores to be done
But I still feel like I have nothing else to do.
I hear cars from the street,
People calling and laughing throughout the
neighborhood
But I still feel like it's all too quiet.
My eyes are wide open
Still, everywhere I look, it's pitch black.
Everything's a blur,
And I know not where my feet are taking me.
I'm just wandering around aimlessly
Without paying any mind to anything
Without a single thought in my somewhat
broken mind.

The Moment of Emptiness

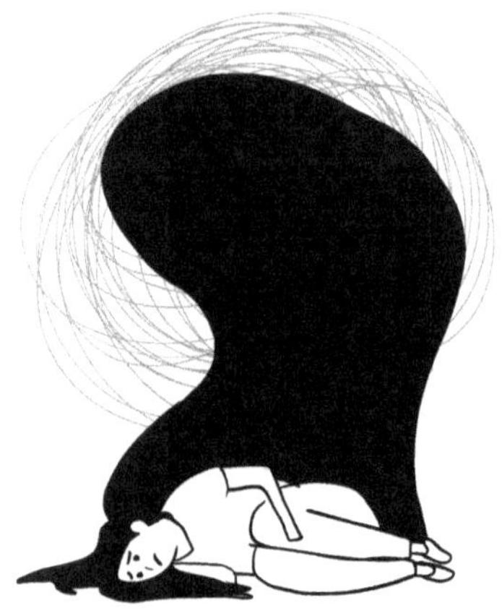

I sit and stare blankly at the wall.
The ticking of the clock,
The only thing that could be heard.
The neighborhood is quiet.
The house feels empty,
And so does the heart and mind.

It's amusing, isn't it?
For it was only a few seconds ago
That I was flooded with emotions
And am caught between laughter and tears
But now I find myself sitting
Staring at an empty wall
Just waiting for the time to pass me by.

Trying Not To Regret

I cried.
I still cry,
Even though I was the one who said goodbye.
Indeed, I was the one to leave,
But I had no other choice,
But to try to choose me.
This game of push and pull, you choose to play
Though fun, it may seem
Is actually not.
The only thing it does
Is leave me wondering if I did something wrong
Or said something I shouldn't,
And it's not fun.
It only leaves my heart in pieces,
And my mind to think of you being with
someone else.

The Seasons of Life

Oh! How fast the time flies
One moment, you're in the middle of Winter
Celebrating the most beautiful holiday of all,
And the next, you're already in Spring
Watching the flower buds as they begin to
bloom.
Then, in the blink of an eye
You find yourself in the middle of the Summer
rain,
The sunny, clear skies and several boiling days.
Soon, it will be Autumn, and the leaves begin to
wither.
There's warmth in the air, yet the Winter breeze
is felt after each passing day.
And then, before we know it, we're back to the
season of holidays,
The cold Winter nights when there's music and
laughter
And when everyone awaits the joy the season
brings
Through family and friends who are, oh, so dear.

Music and Memories

I listen to music to get my mind off things,
But the problem is that every song I listen to
Either reminds me of something or someone.
Certain types of music sometimes reminds me of
a loved one
A friend, a family member or sometimes
It reminds me of something that I desperately
want to forget.

Music does help me get my mind off things,
But most of the time, it takes me back to places I
want to forget,
It takes me back to the first time I met someone,
And sometimes to the last time we spoke.
This, in turn, only leaves me in a state of
constant mixed emotions,
Sitting alone in my room, contemplating life.

www.ingramcontent.com/pod-product-compliance
Lightning Source LLC
LaVergne TN
LVHW050921200726
843508LV00011B/2247